BODY WORKS

by **Janine Wheeler**

Illustrated with photographs

Drawings by **Christy Krames**

HAMPTON-BROWN

Parts of the Body

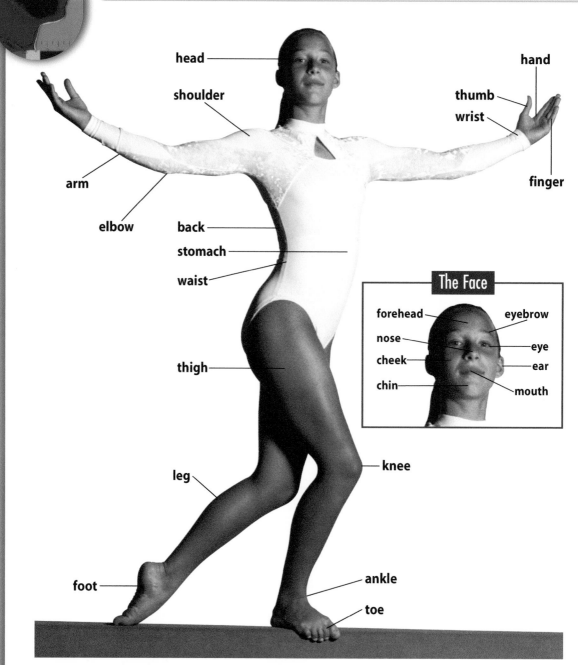

head

shoulder

hand

thumb

wrist

arm

finger

elbow

back

stomach

waist

The Face

forehead

eyebrow

nose

eye

cheek

ear

chin

mouth

thigh

knee

leg

foot

ankle

toe

The Heart

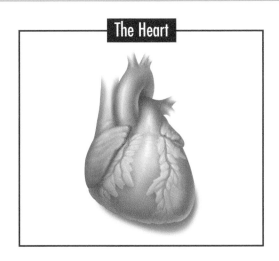

The Lungs

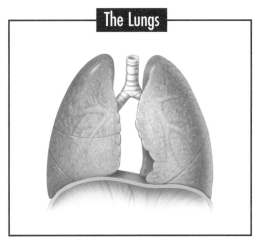

The Skeleton

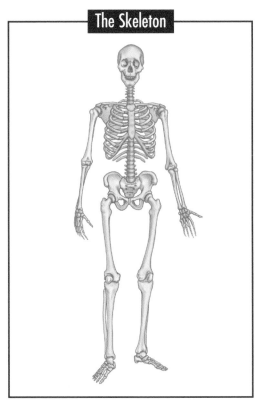

The Muscles

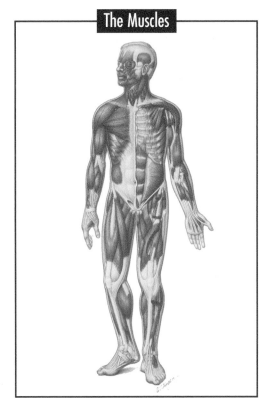

BODY WORKS

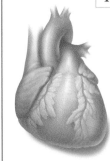

THE SKELETON

You work your body hard.
What makes your body work?

The skeleton helps your body work. The skeleton is the body's frame. It gives the body shape.

A helmet and pads protect this woman's bones when she is skating.

The Skeleton

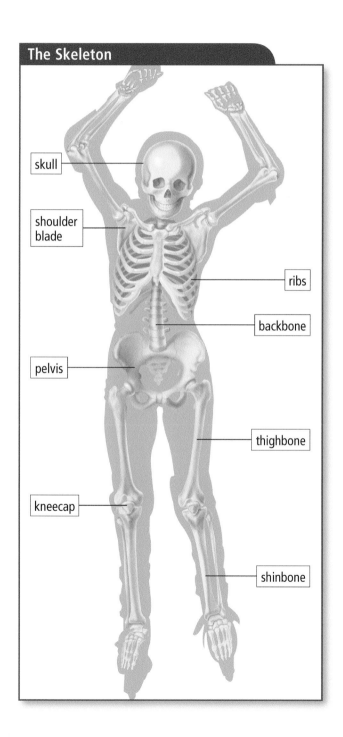

skull

shoulder blade

ribs

backbone

pelvis

thighbone

kneecap

shinbone

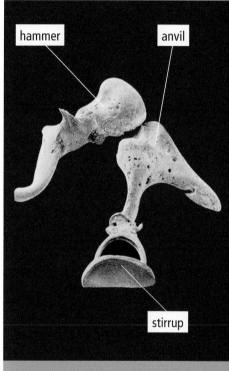

hammer

anvil

stirrup

The smallest bones are in your ear. The stirrup bone is only this long:

↑
1/8"

7

THE MUSCLES

Muscles help your body work. Most muscles work with your bones. They pull the bones to make them move.

This rowing team uses many muscles to pull the boat forward.

Muscle Contraction

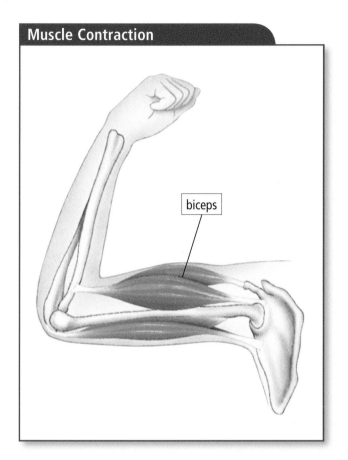

biceps

When this muscle, the biceps, contracts, or gets shorter, it pulls up the arm.

You use 17 muscles to smile.

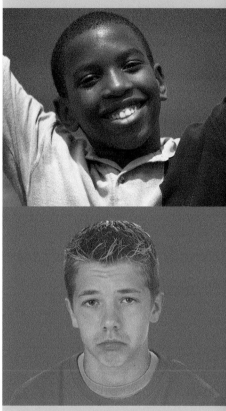

You use 43 muscles to frown.

9

THE HEART

The heart is a special muscle. The heart helps your body work. It pumps blood to all parts of the body.

Exercise makes the heart beat faster.

How Fast Does Your Heart Beat?

Put two fingers on the inside of your wrist, below your thumb. You should feel a beat, called your pulse. Count the number of beats in 10 seconds. Multiply it by six. That is the number of times your heart beats in one minute.

THE BLOOD

Blood helps your body work. Blood takes oxygen to all parts of the body. It takes away carbon dioxide and other waste.

When you run, your heart beats faster to pump more blood. The blood takes more oxygen to the body. Then the body can work harder.

Circulatory System

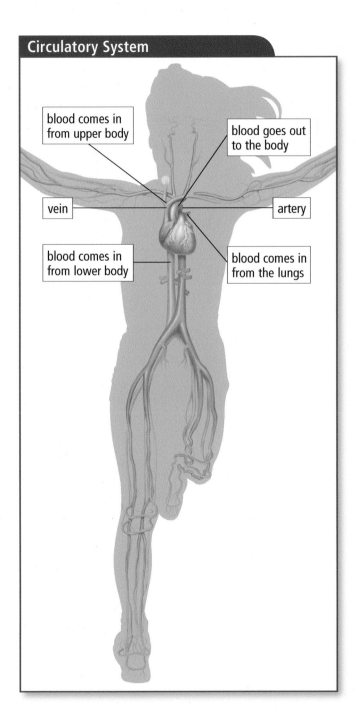

blood comes in from upper body

blood goes out to the body

vein

artery

blood comes in from lower body

blood comes in from the lungs

40 Quarts

When you run, your heart may beat 100 or more times per minute. It can pump up to 40 quarts of blood a minute.

THE LUNGS

Lungs help your body work. Lungs breathe in oxygen. They release carbon dioxide.

Swimmers need strong lungs to hold their breath while they are underwater.

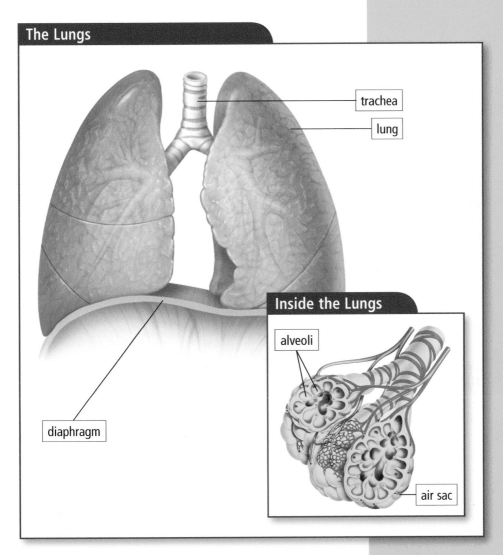

The Lungs

trachea

lung

diaphragm

Inside the Lungs

alveoli

air sac

The trachea, or windpipe, branches into two tubes. These tubes then branch into thousands of smaller tubes. At the end of the smallest tubes are clusters of alveoli called air sacs. There are about 300 million air sacs in your lungs.

THE NERVOUS SYSTEM

The nervous system helps your body work.
It takes messages to and from the brain.

The soccer player sees a ball coming.
The nerves send a message. They tell
the brain what the eyes see. The brain
tells the body what to do.

The Nervous System

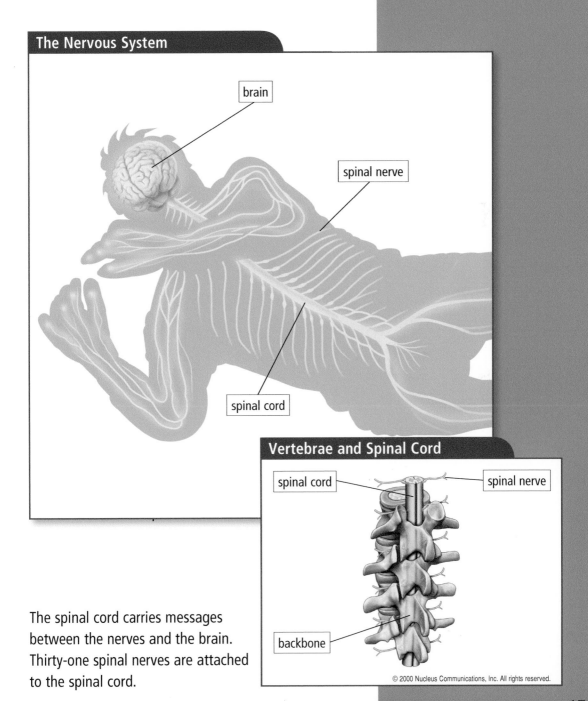

brain

spinal nerve

spinal cord

Vertebrae and Spinal Cord

spinal cord

spinal nerve

backbone

The spinal cord carries messages between the nerves and the brain. Thirty-one spinal nerves are attached to the spinal cord.

THE BRAIN

Your brain helps your body work. Different centers in the brain control how you think, feel, and move. The brain also controls other body systems.

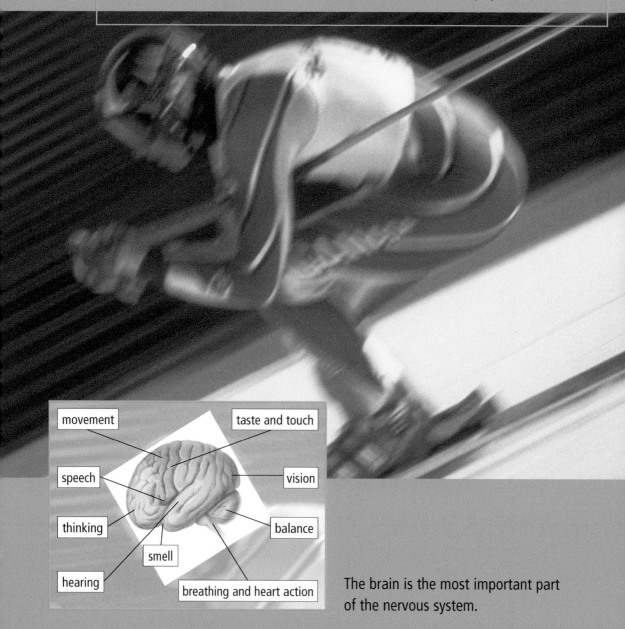

movement

taste and touch

speech

vision

thinking

balance

smell

hearing

breathing and heart action

The brain is the most important part of the nervous system.

THE SENSES

The five senses help your body work. Your senses help you see, hear, smell, taste, and touch. The nerves carry sense messages to the brain.

Skin touches and feels.

Eyes see.

Ears hear.

The nose smells.

The tongue tastes.

KEEP YOUR BODY CLEAN

Healthy habits help your body work.

Keep clean to kill germs that make you sick.

EAT HEALTHY FOODS

Healthy foods give the body energy.

They have lots of vitamins.

MyPyramid.gov
STEPS TO A HEALTHIER YOU

Grains	**Vegetables**	**Fruits**	**Fats**	**Milk**	**Meat & Beans**
Make half your grains whole	*Vary your vegetables*	*Focus on fruits*	*Use sparingly*	*Get your calcium-rich foods*	*Go lean with protein*

KEEP ACTIVE

Exercise your body. Exercise strengthens your heart, lungs, and muscles. It helps your body work better.

GET ENOUGH REST

Quiet activities let your body rest.

Sleeping is the best way to rest your body.

A five-year-old child needs about 12 hours of sleep.
An adult needs about 8 hours of sleep.

GLOSSARY

alveoli: tiny air pockets in the lungs. *The blood gets oxygen in the alveoli.*

beat: a steady rhythm of sound. *The beat of your heart sounds like this: lub-dub, lub-dub, lub-dub.*

carbon dioxide: a gas. *Carbon dioxide is a waste in the blood stream.*

center: a special place. *There are centers in your brain for each of your senses.*

cluster: a group of things that are alike. *Many clusters of alveoli in your lungs help you breathe.*

contract: to get shorter. *When you move your arm, one muscle contracts while another stretches.*

control: to tell what to do. *Your brain helps control your muscles when you move.*

energy: the power you need to move your body. *Food gives your body energy.*

exercise: to move your body. *When you exercise, you make your heart pump faster.*

germ: a small living thing that can make you sick. *Some germs can give you a cold.*

oxygen: a gas found in the air we breathe. *The body needs oxygen to live.*

pulse: a beat you feel in your arteries as your heart pumps. *Your pulse speeds up when your heart beats faster.*

pump: to move fluid. *Your heart pumps blood through your arteries and veins.*

system: parts of the body that work together to do a special job. *Your skeleton is a system of bones.*

vitamin: a natural material found in food that keeps the body healthy. *Some vitamins are made within the body.*

waste: something that is no longer needed. *Carbon dioxide is a waste from your body.*